Test Page

Welcome to your test page! This is a great place to try out your favorite coloring materials and become familiar with the book's paper weight and thickness. You can use it to practice new coloring techniques too!

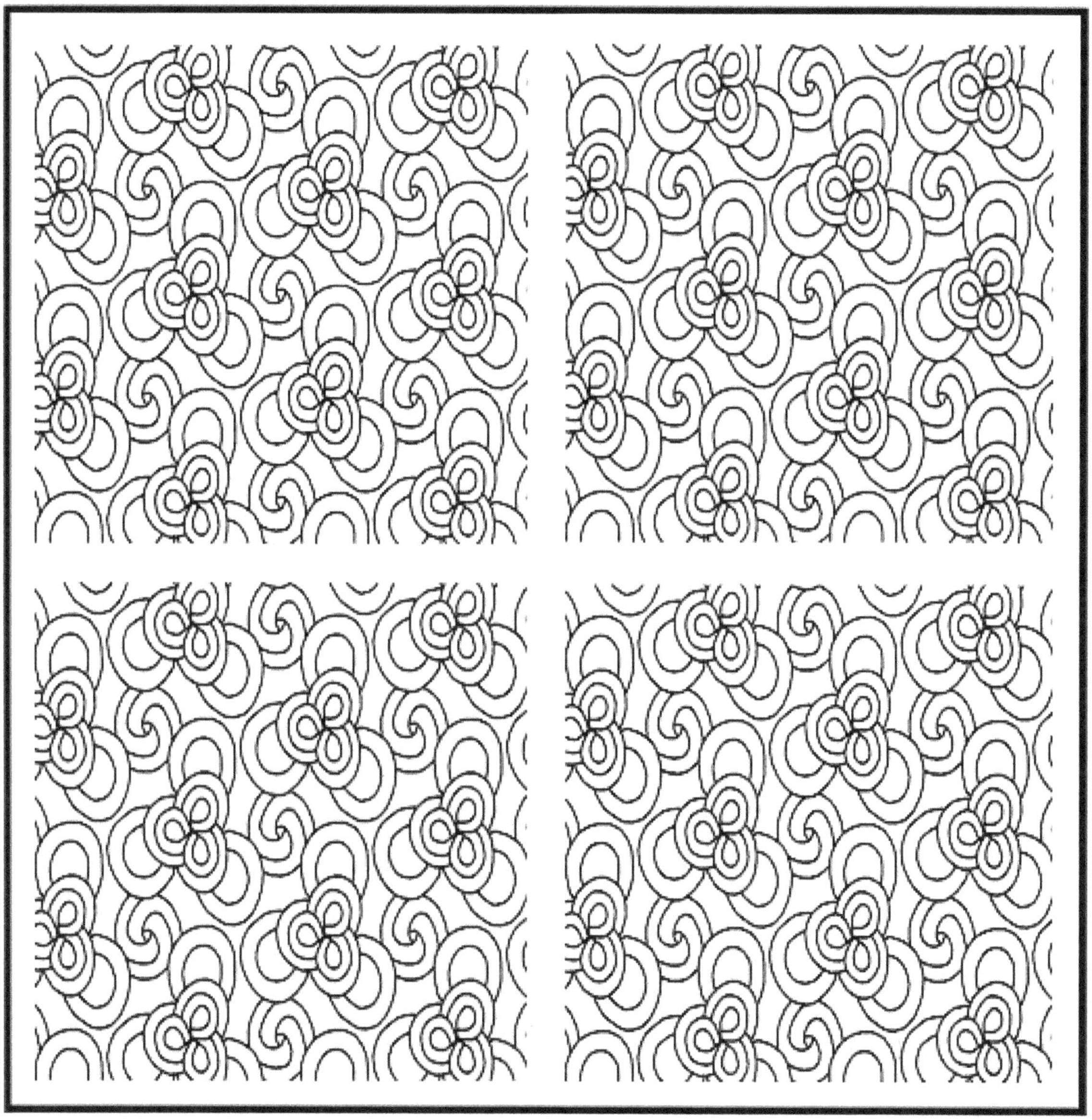

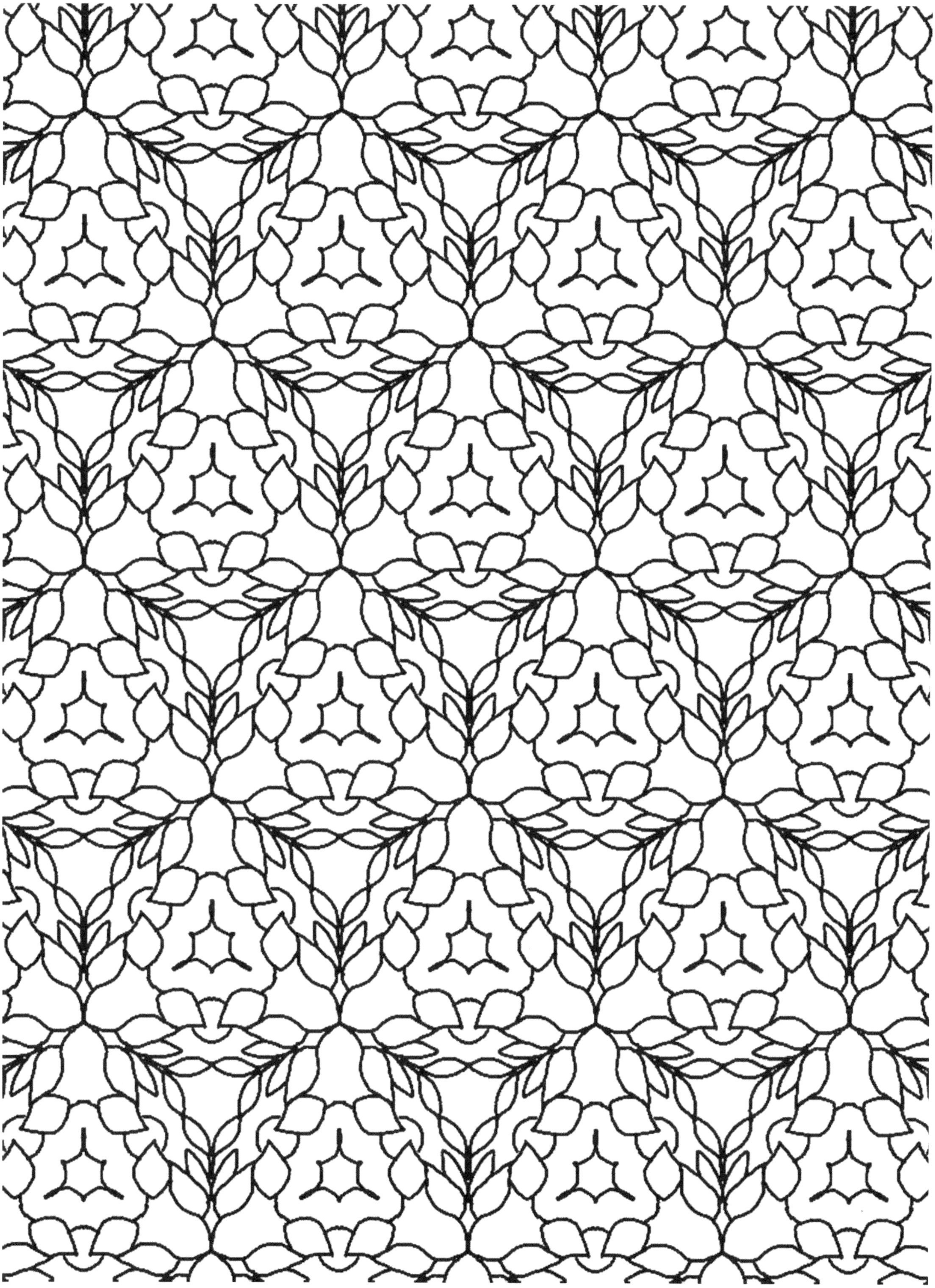

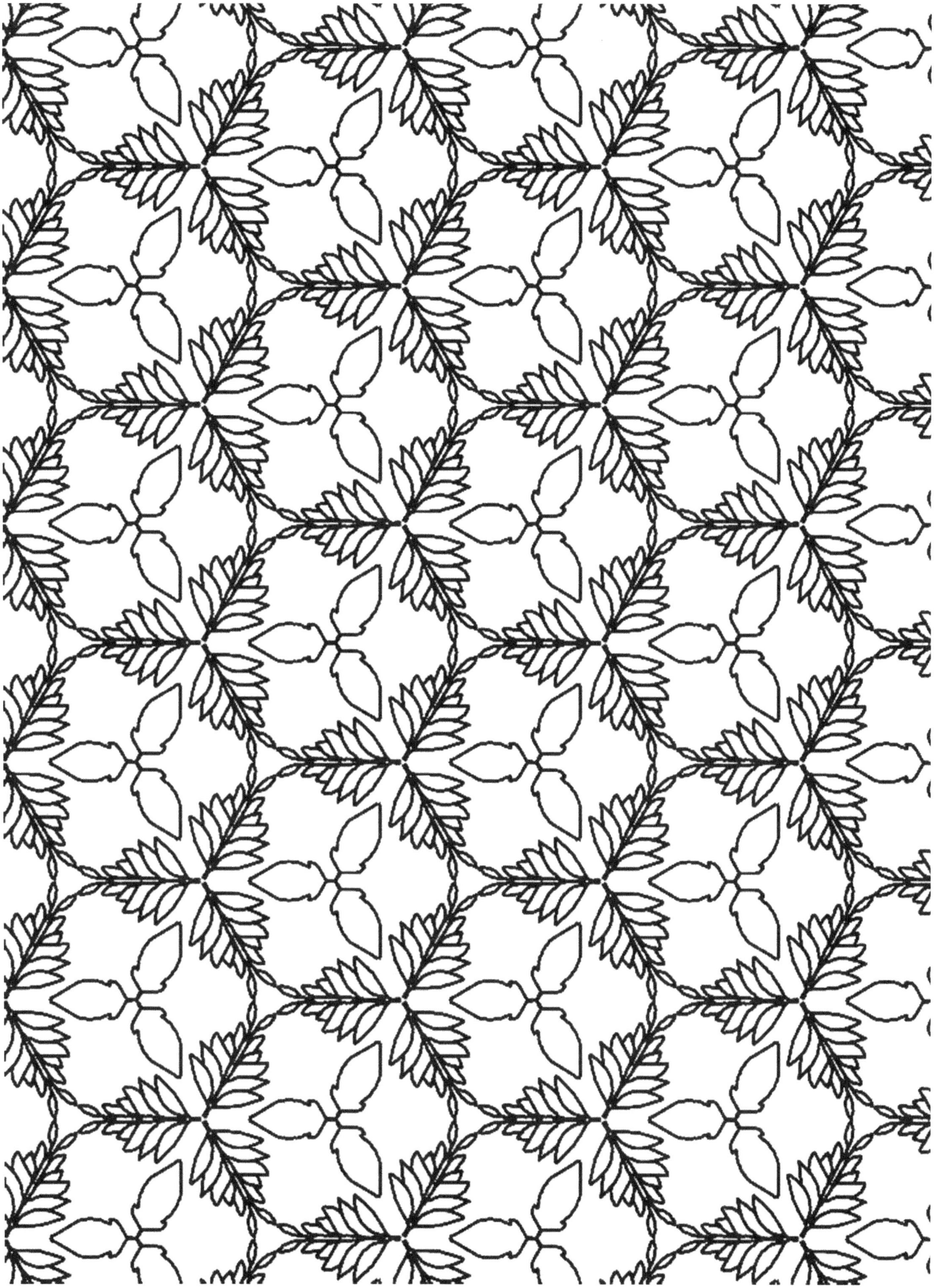

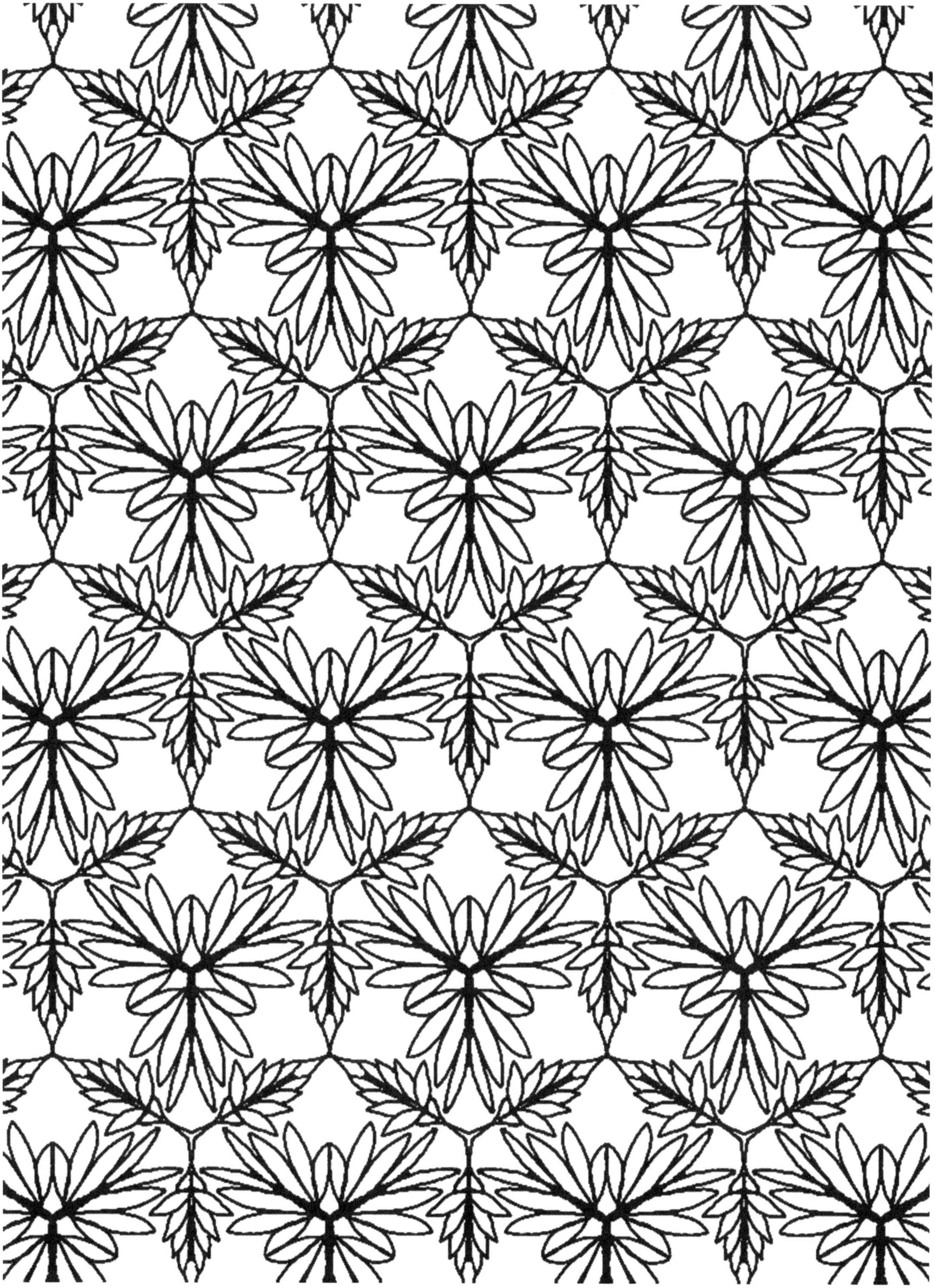

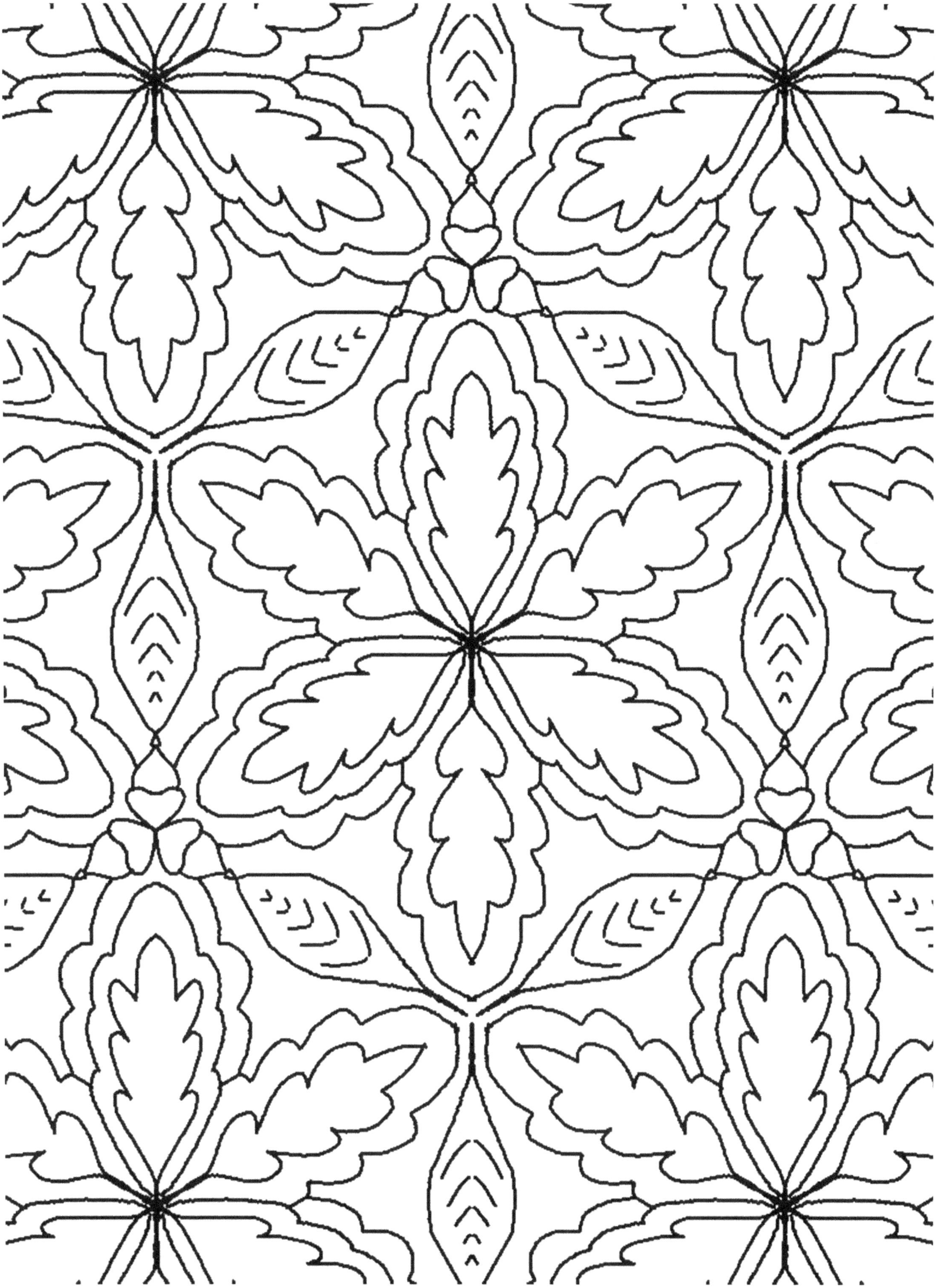

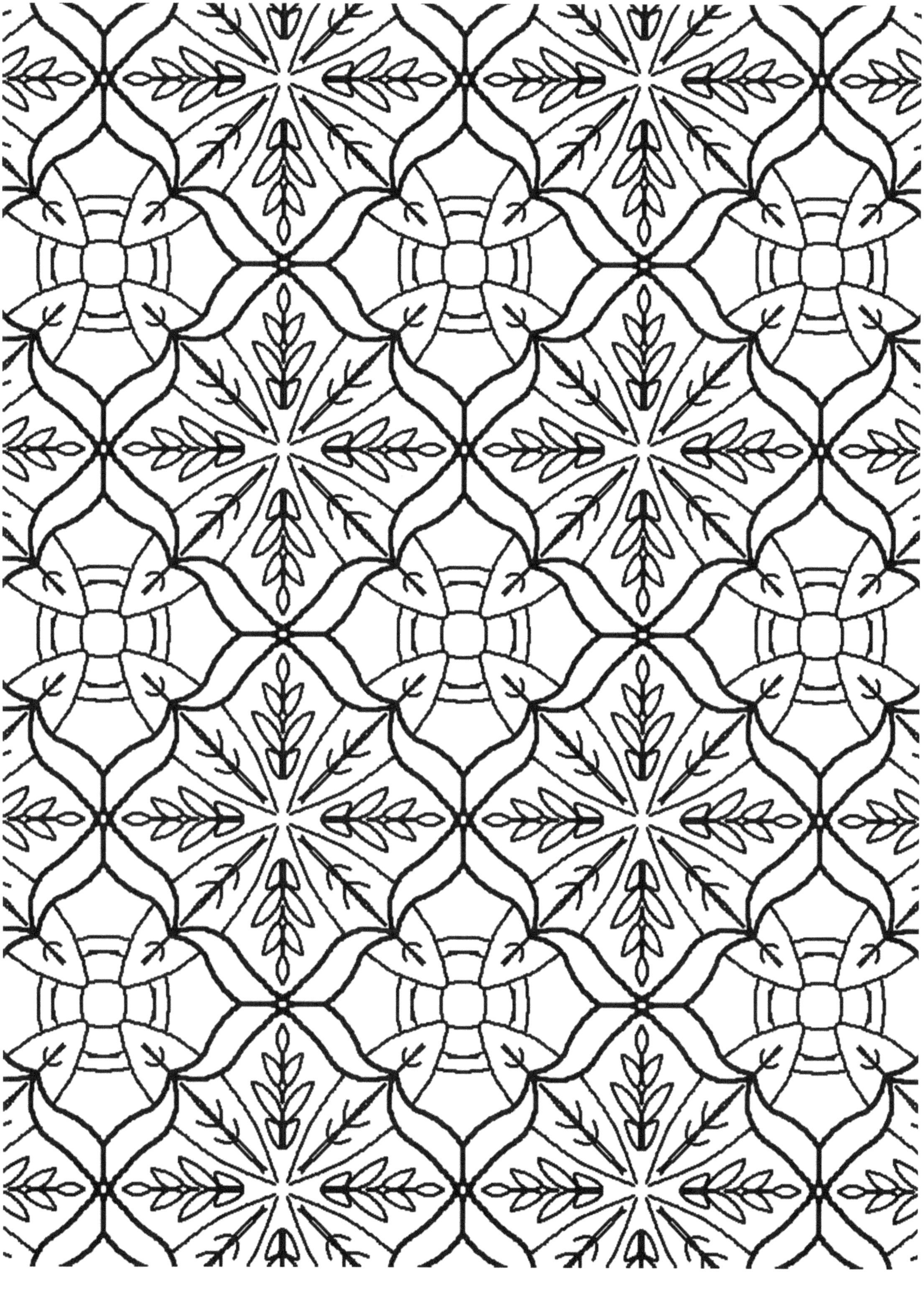

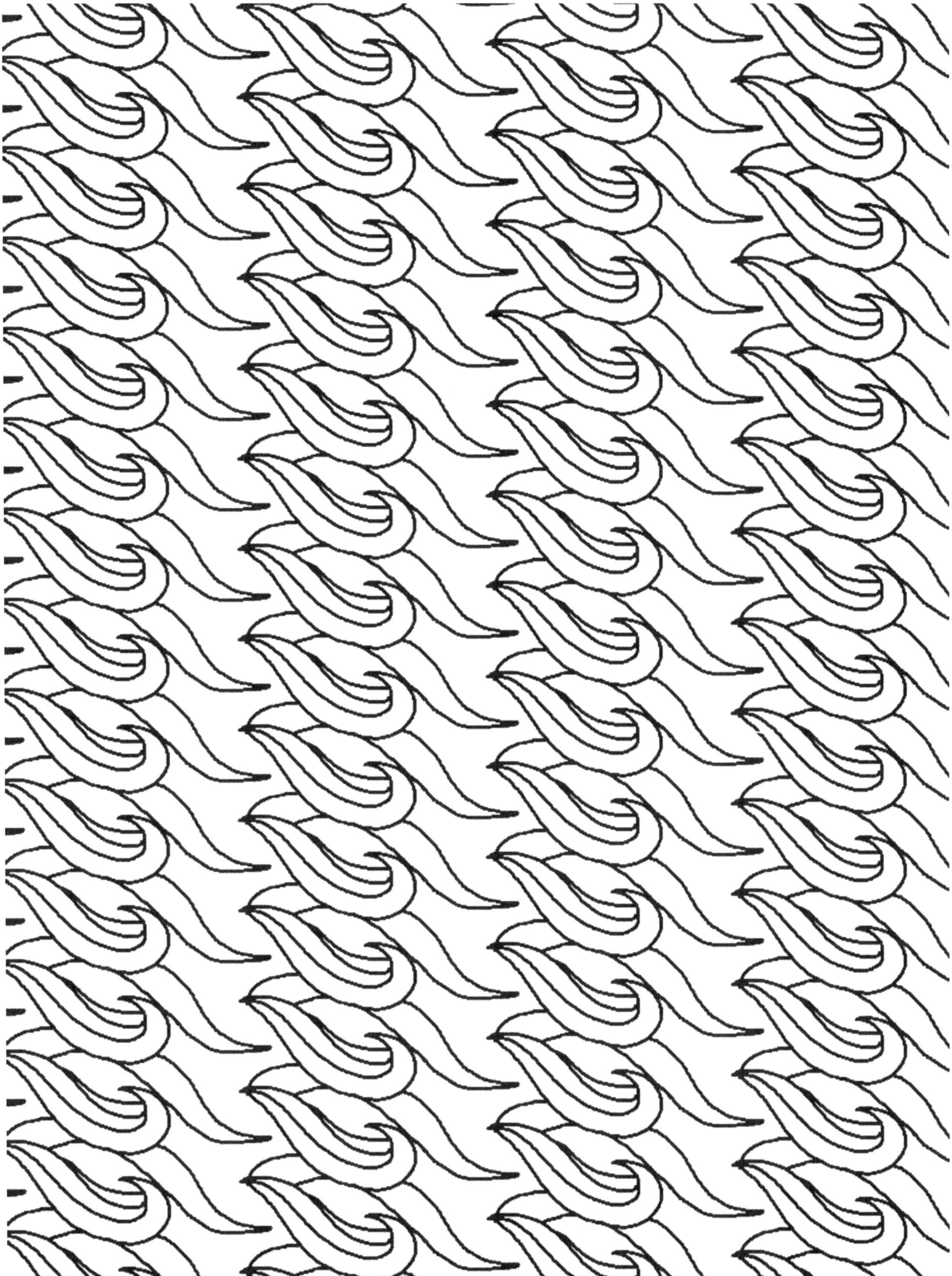

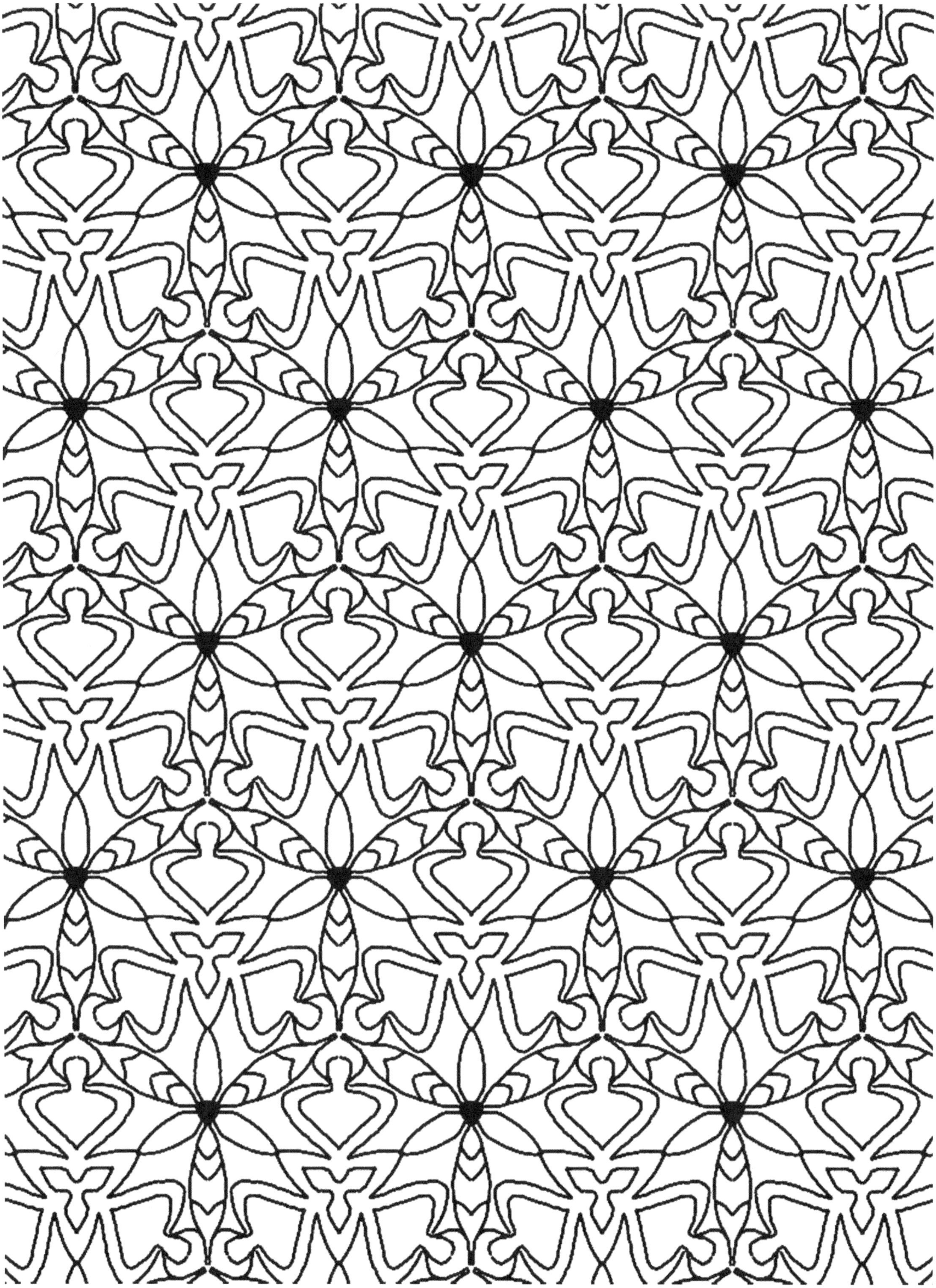

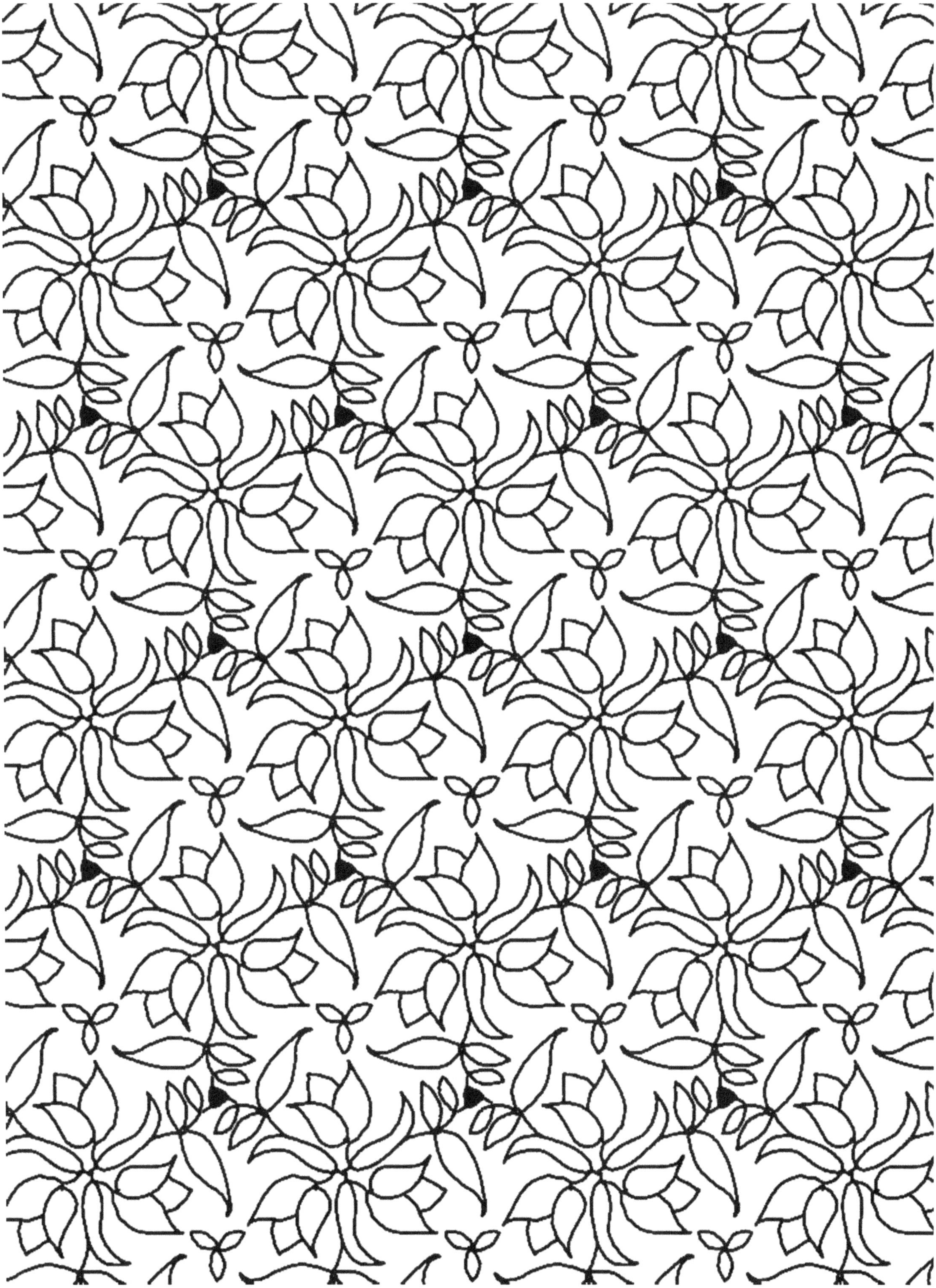

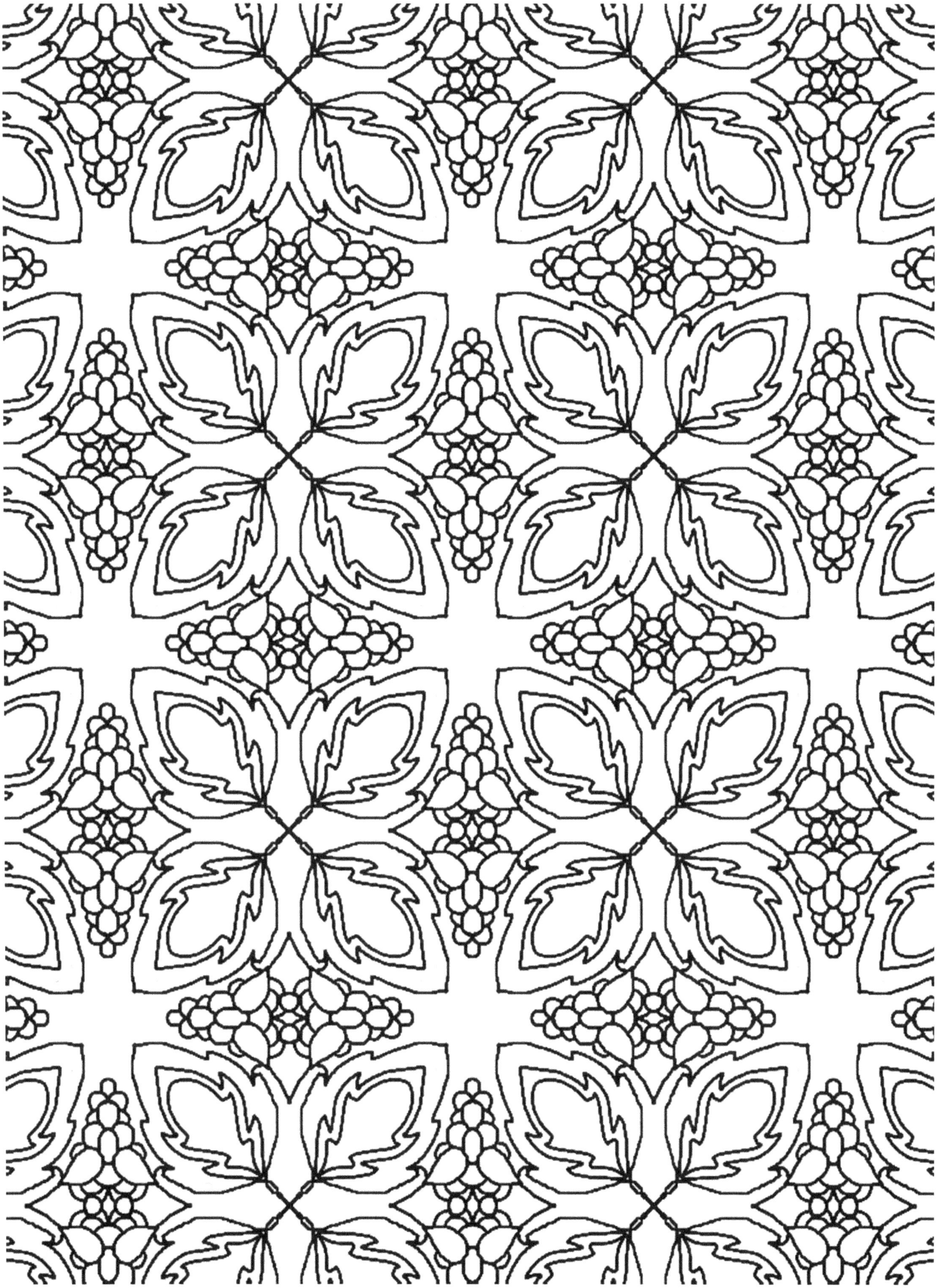

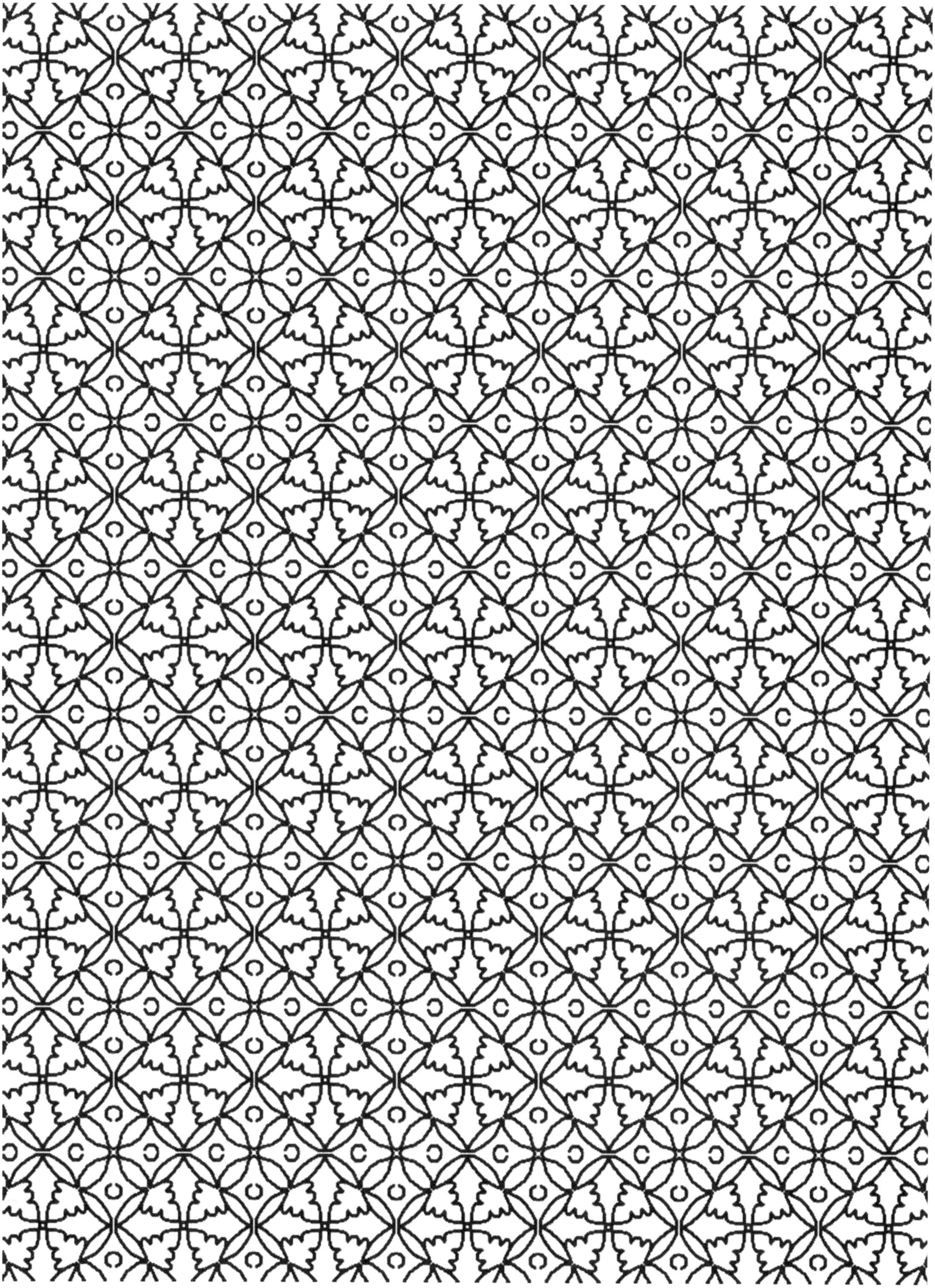

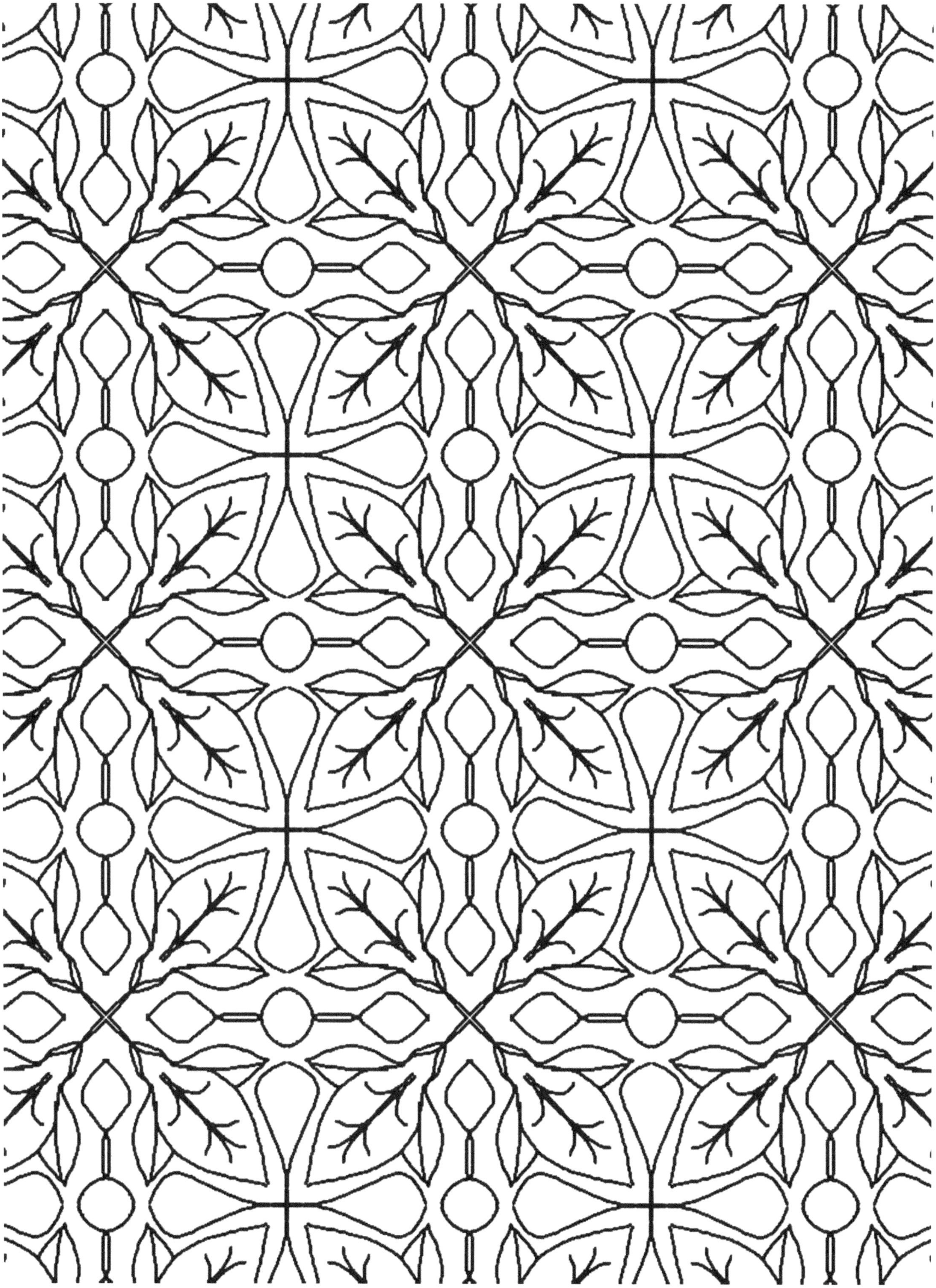

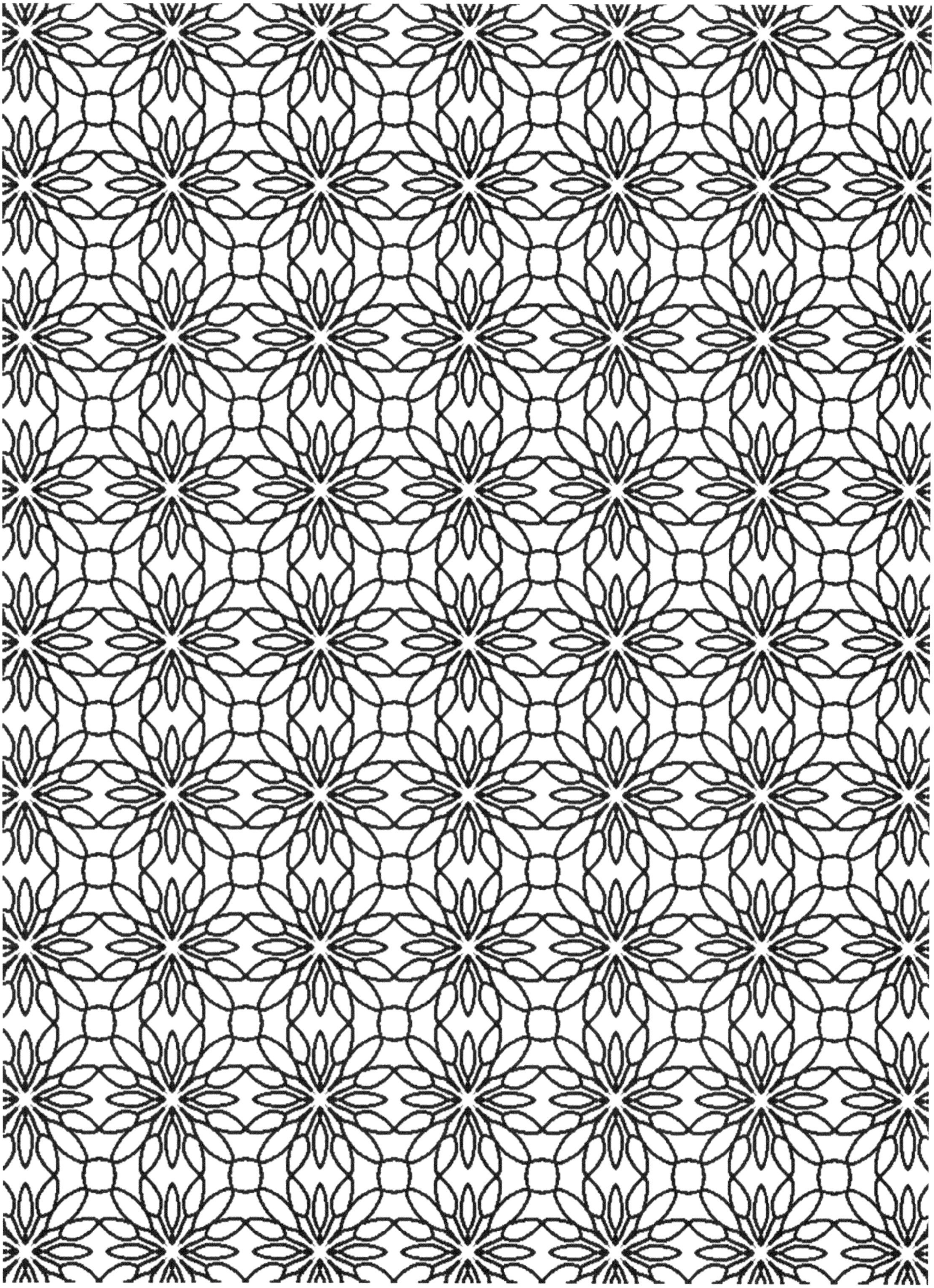

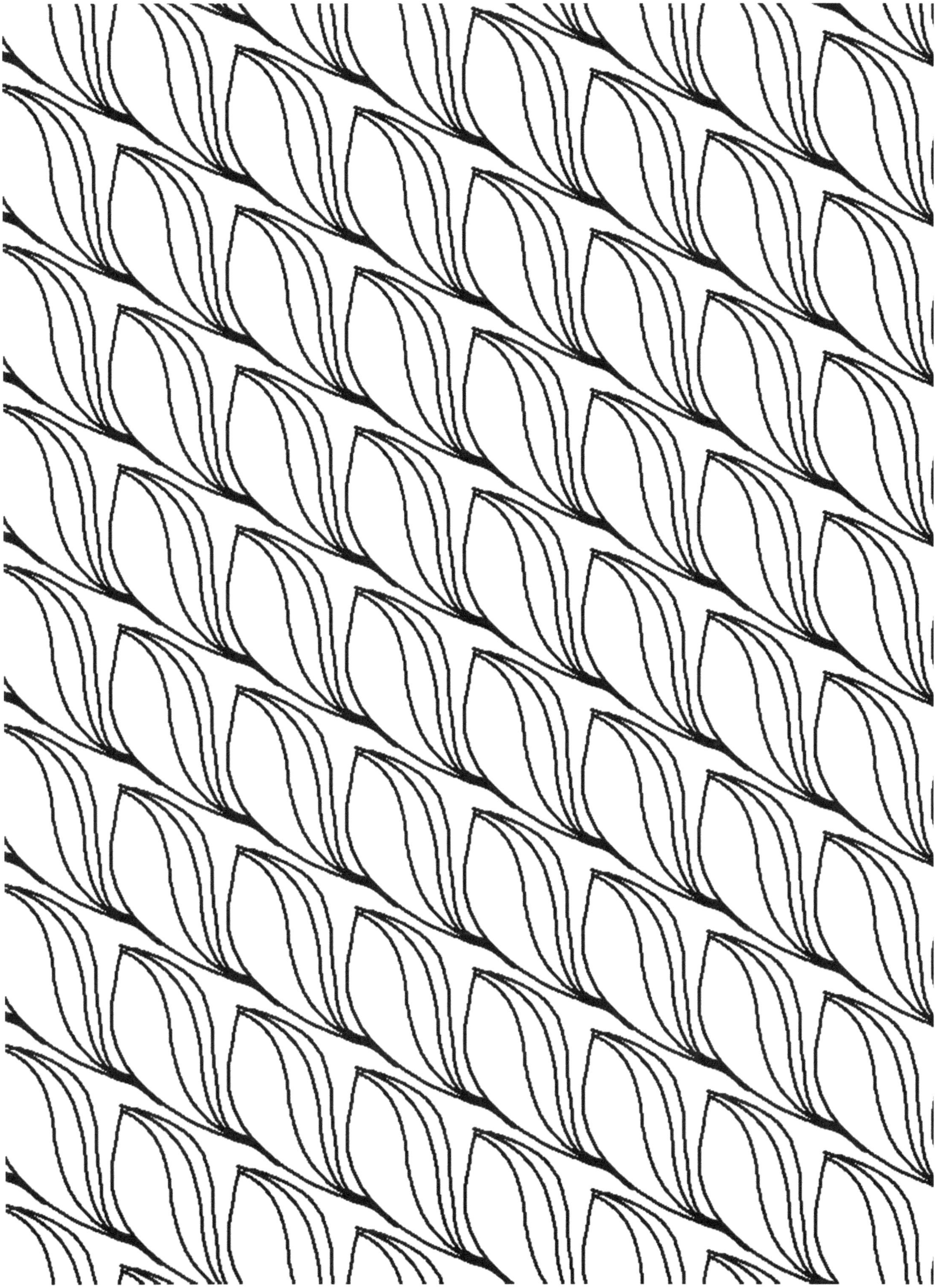

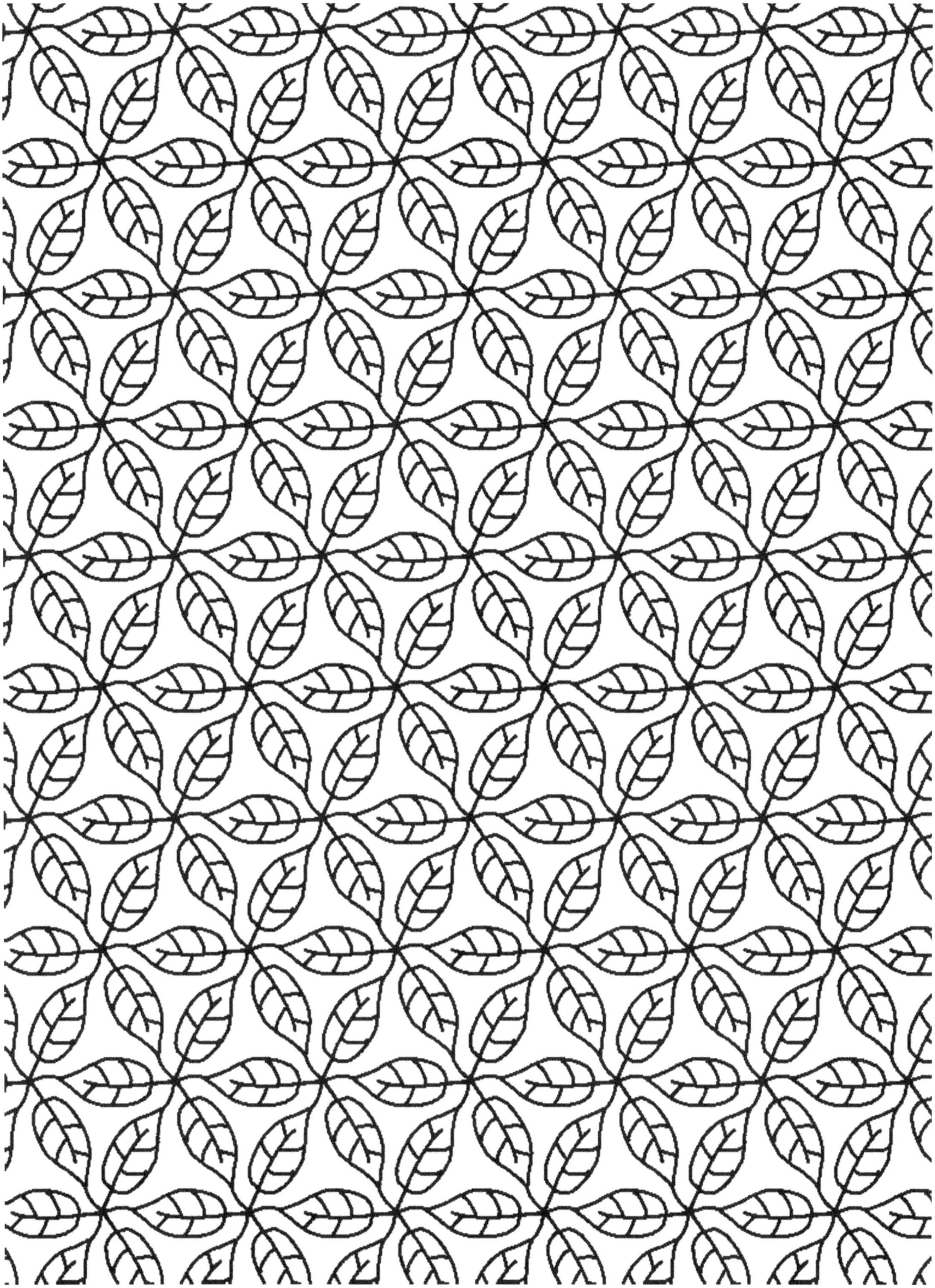

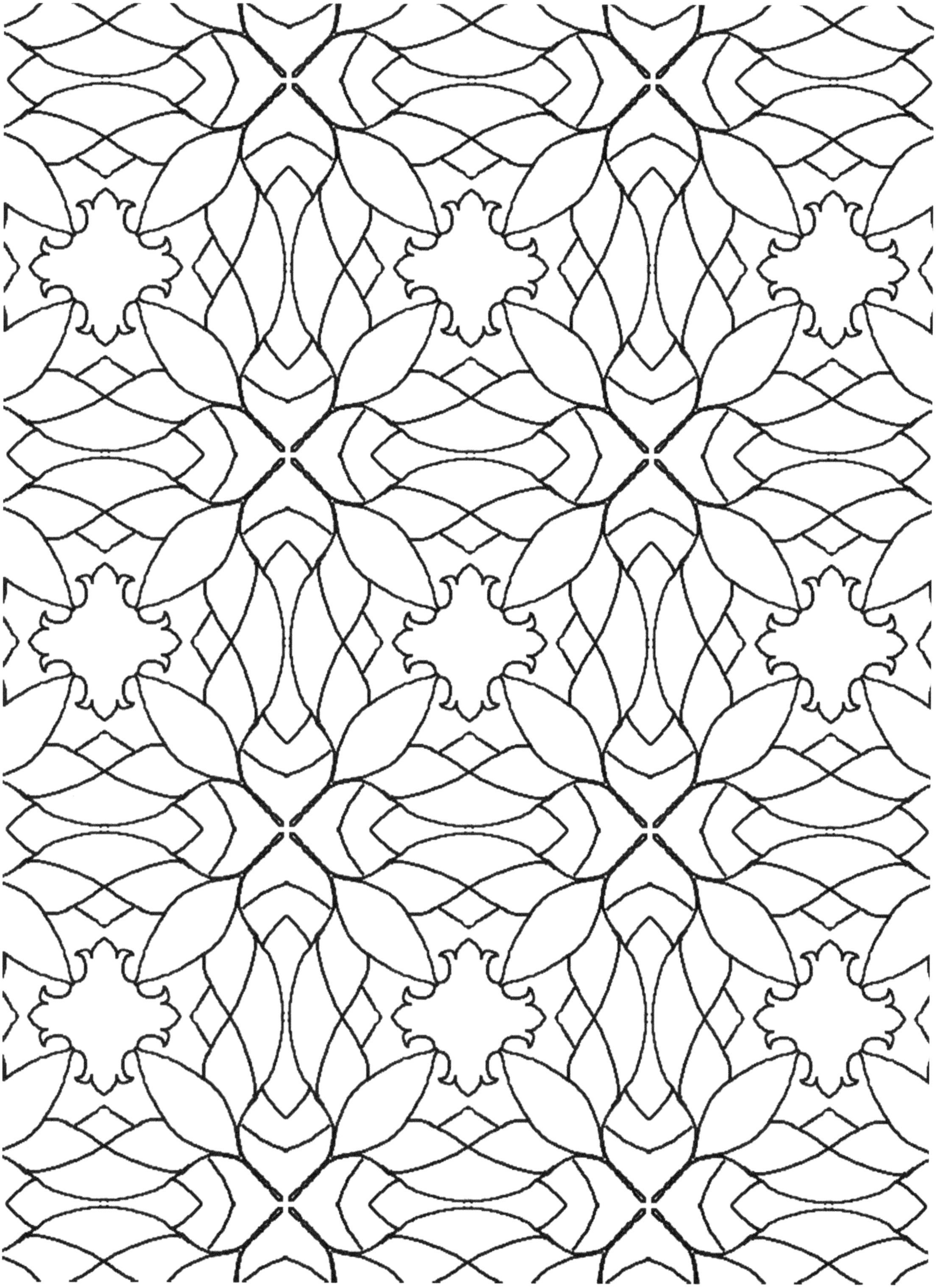

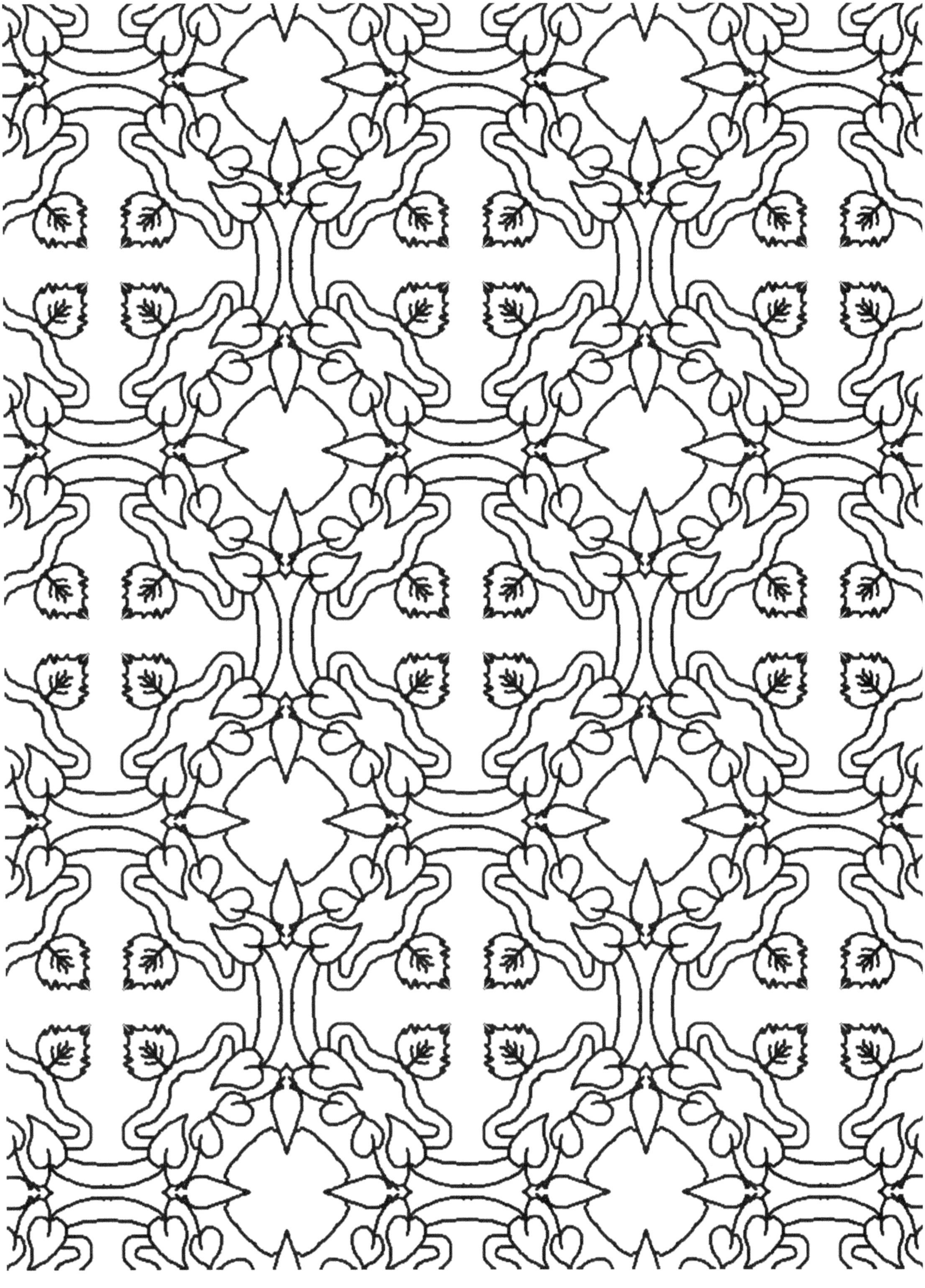

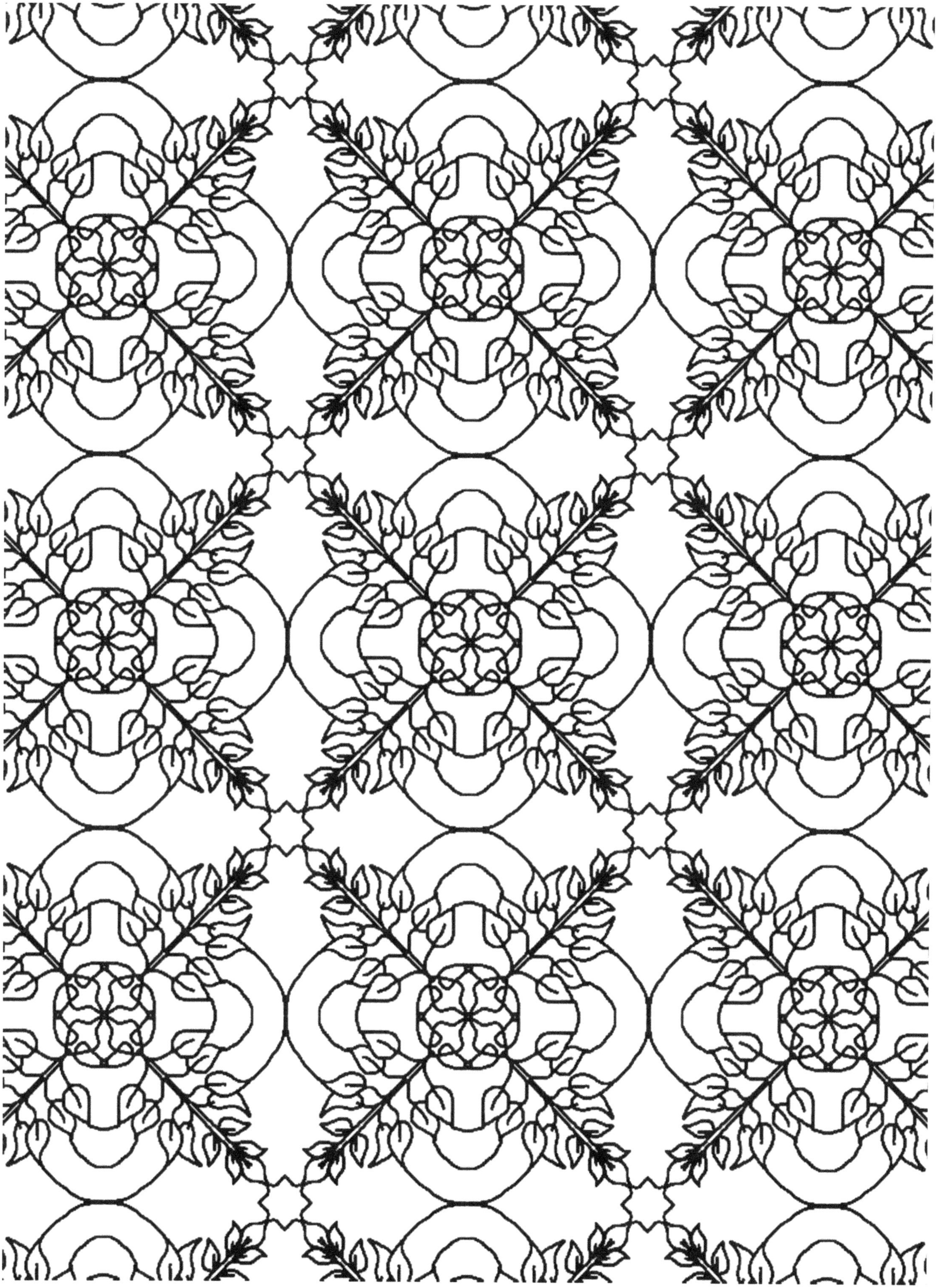

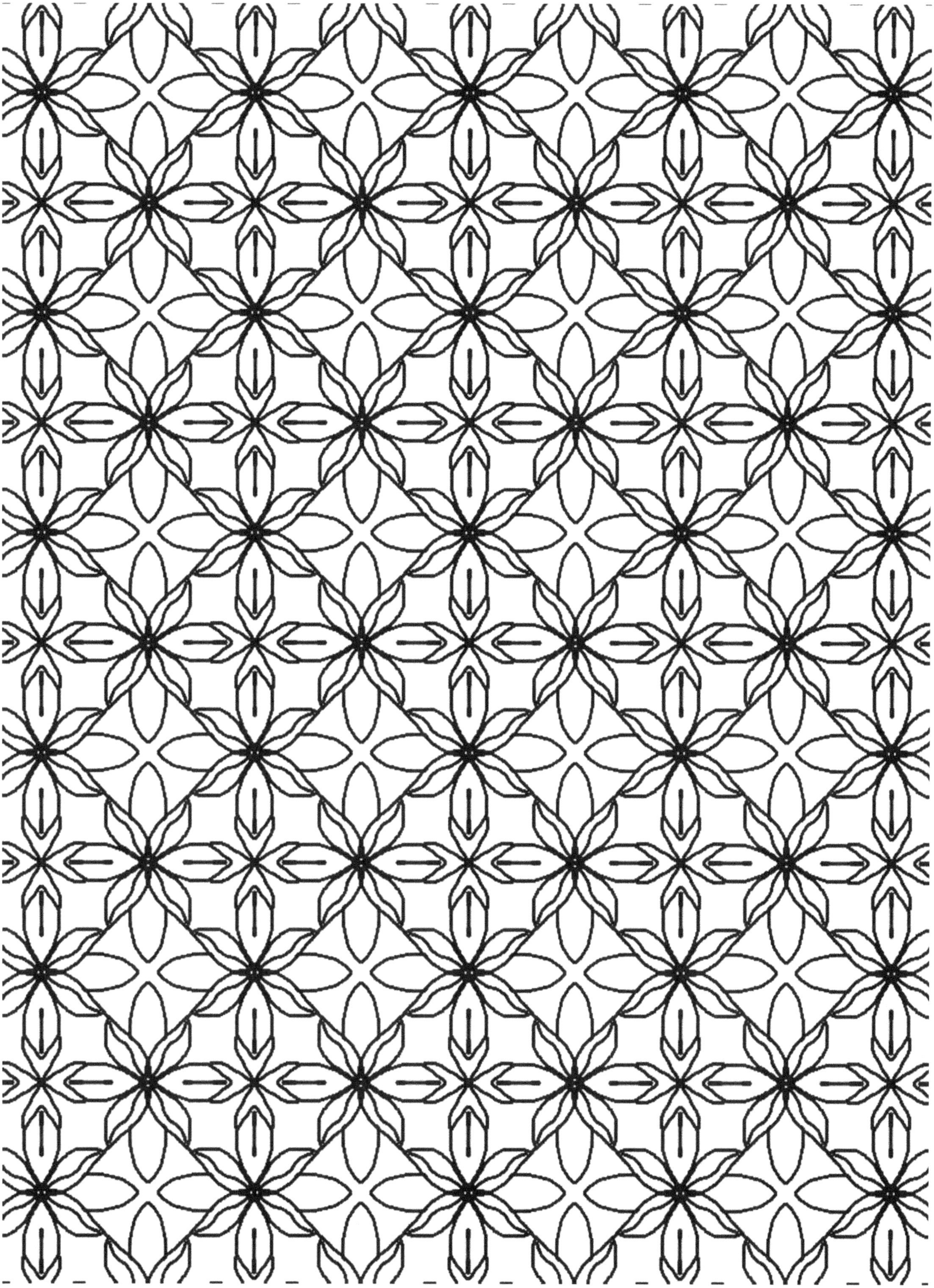

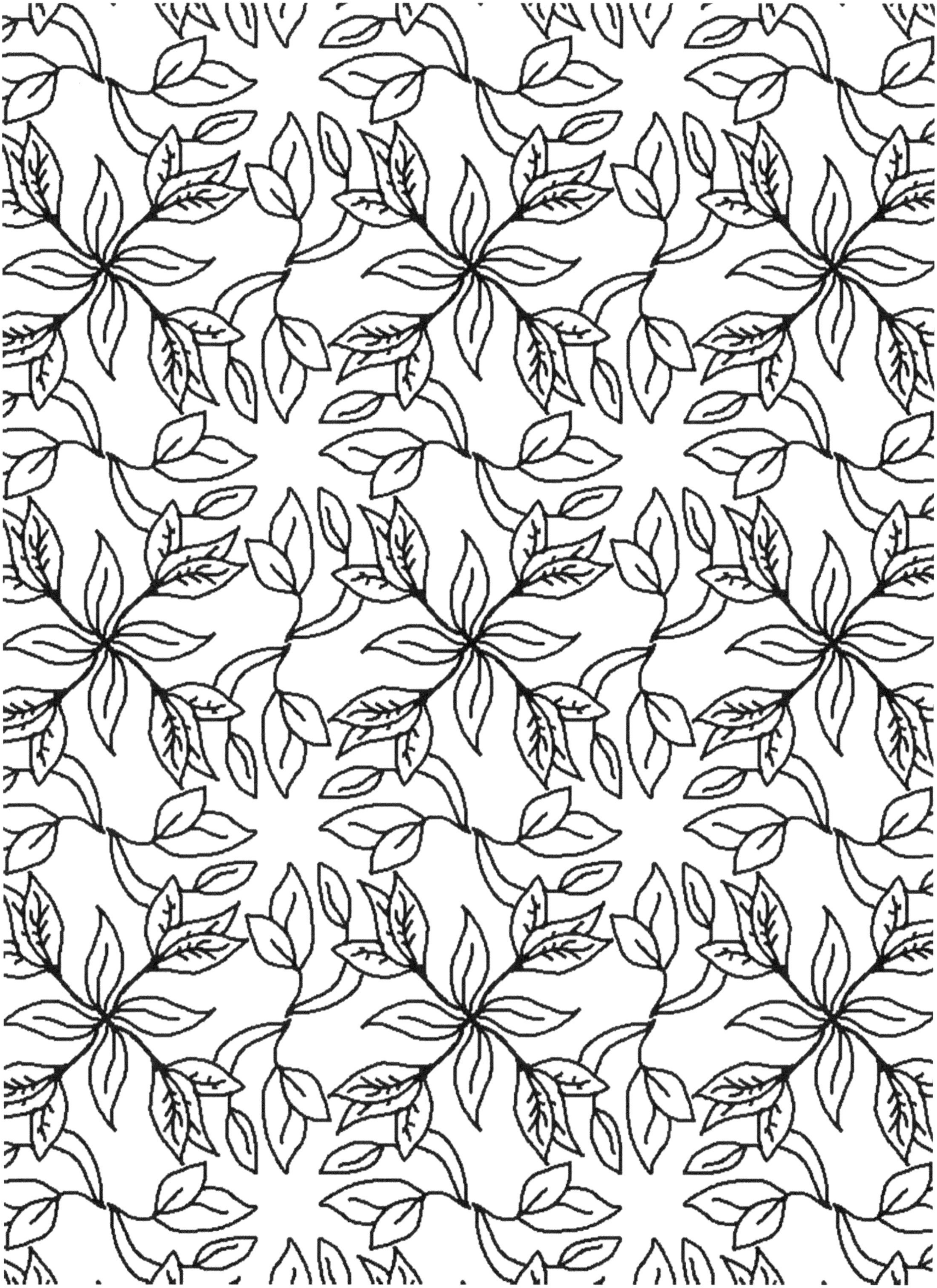

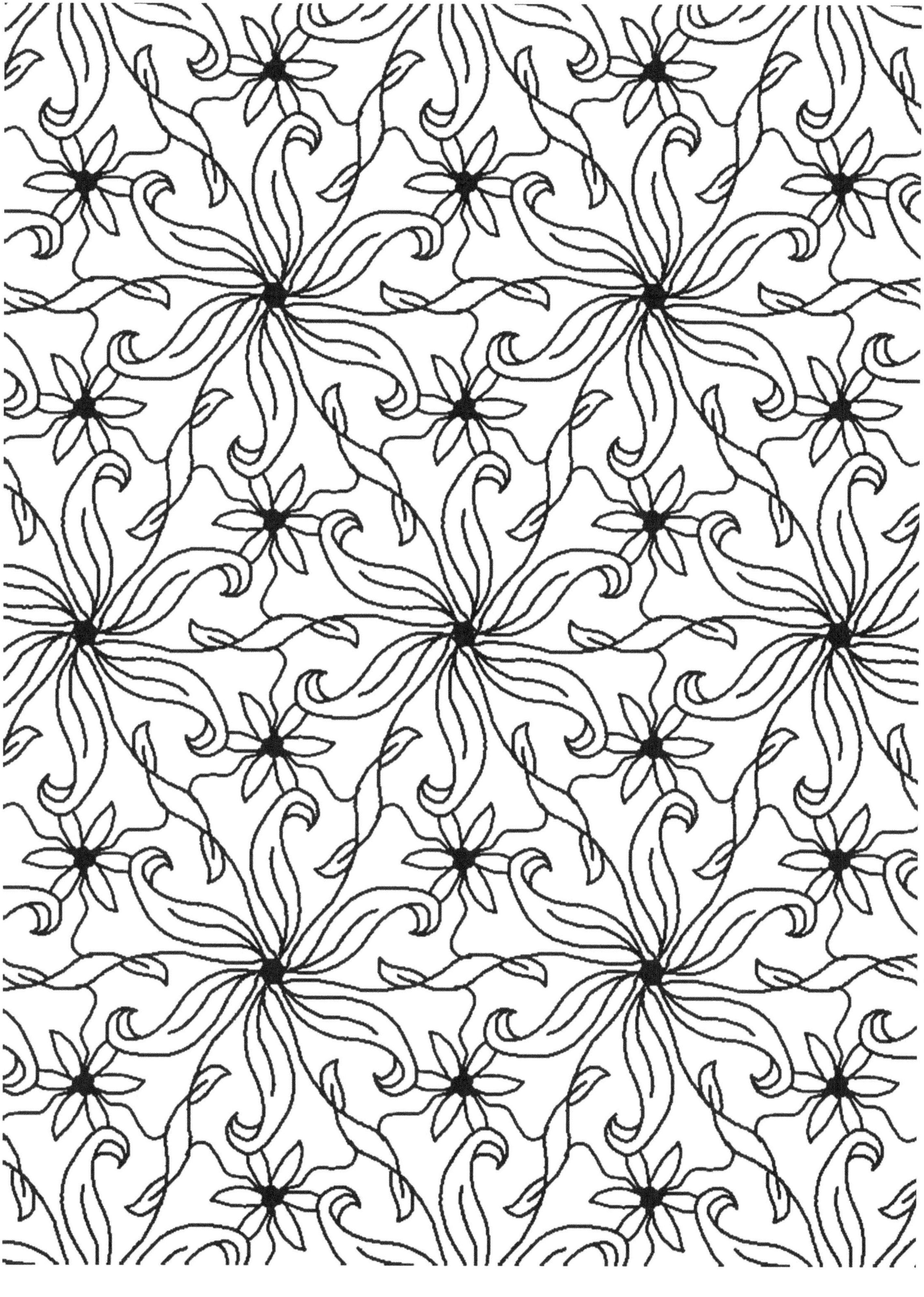

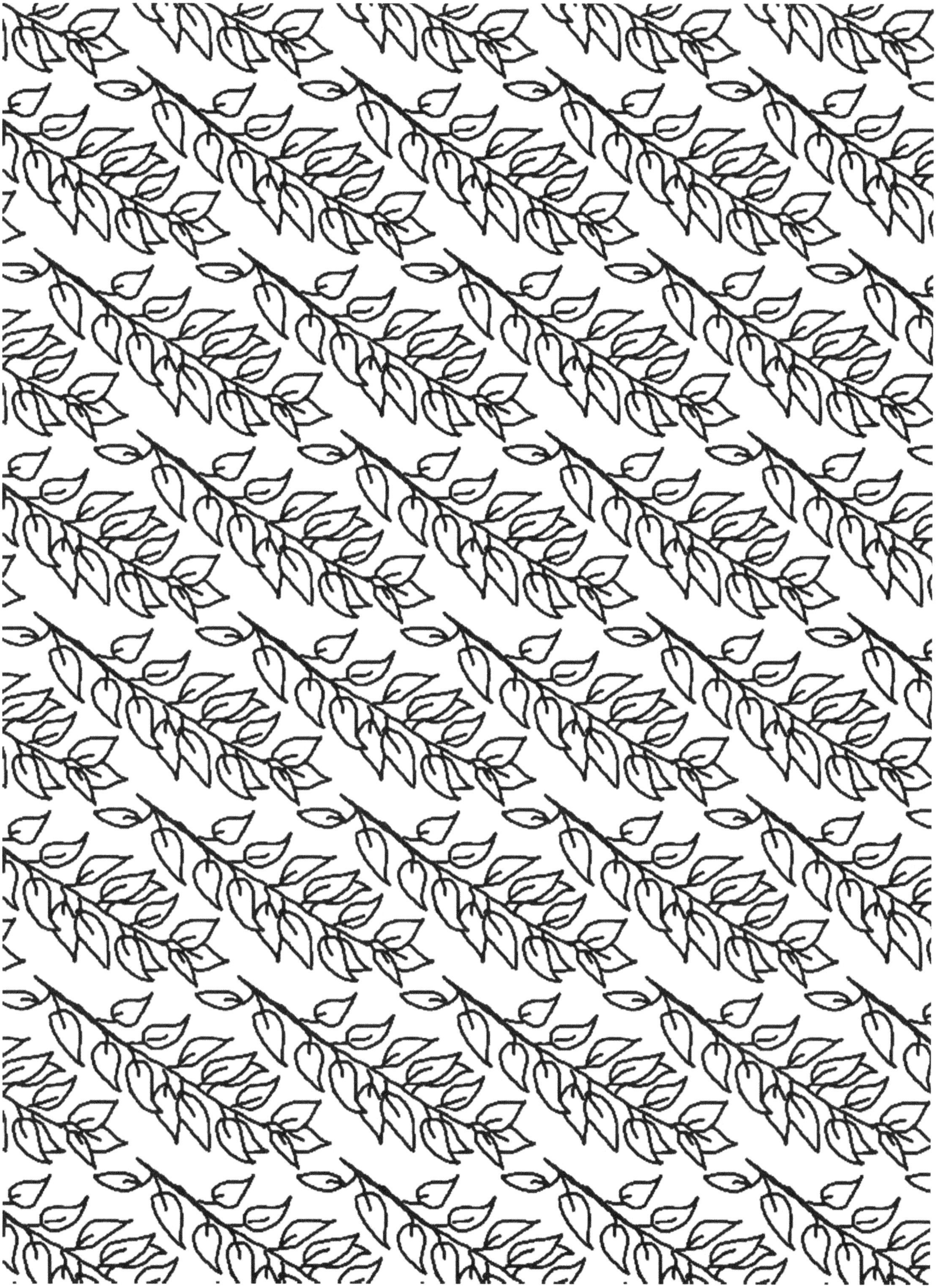

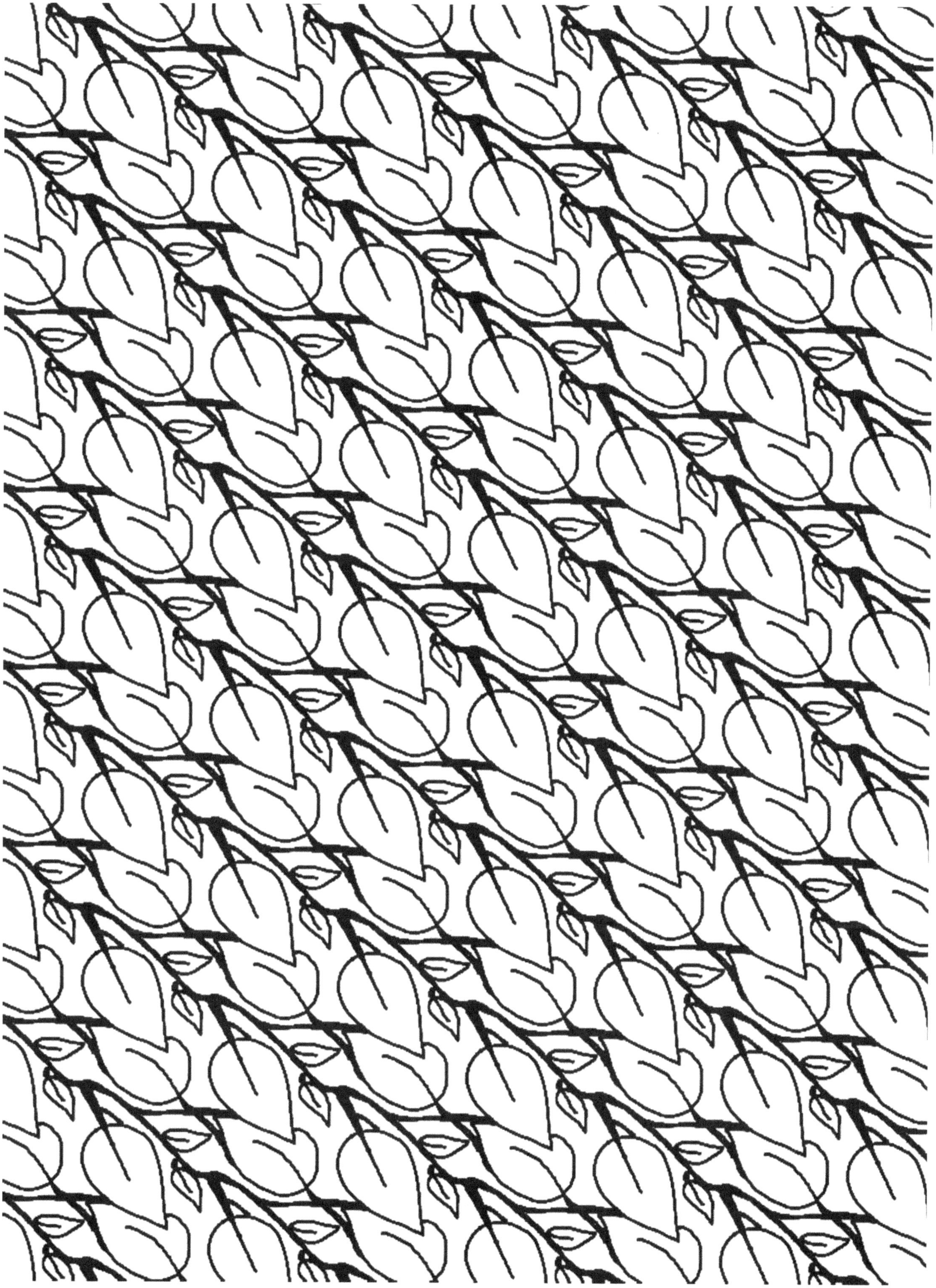

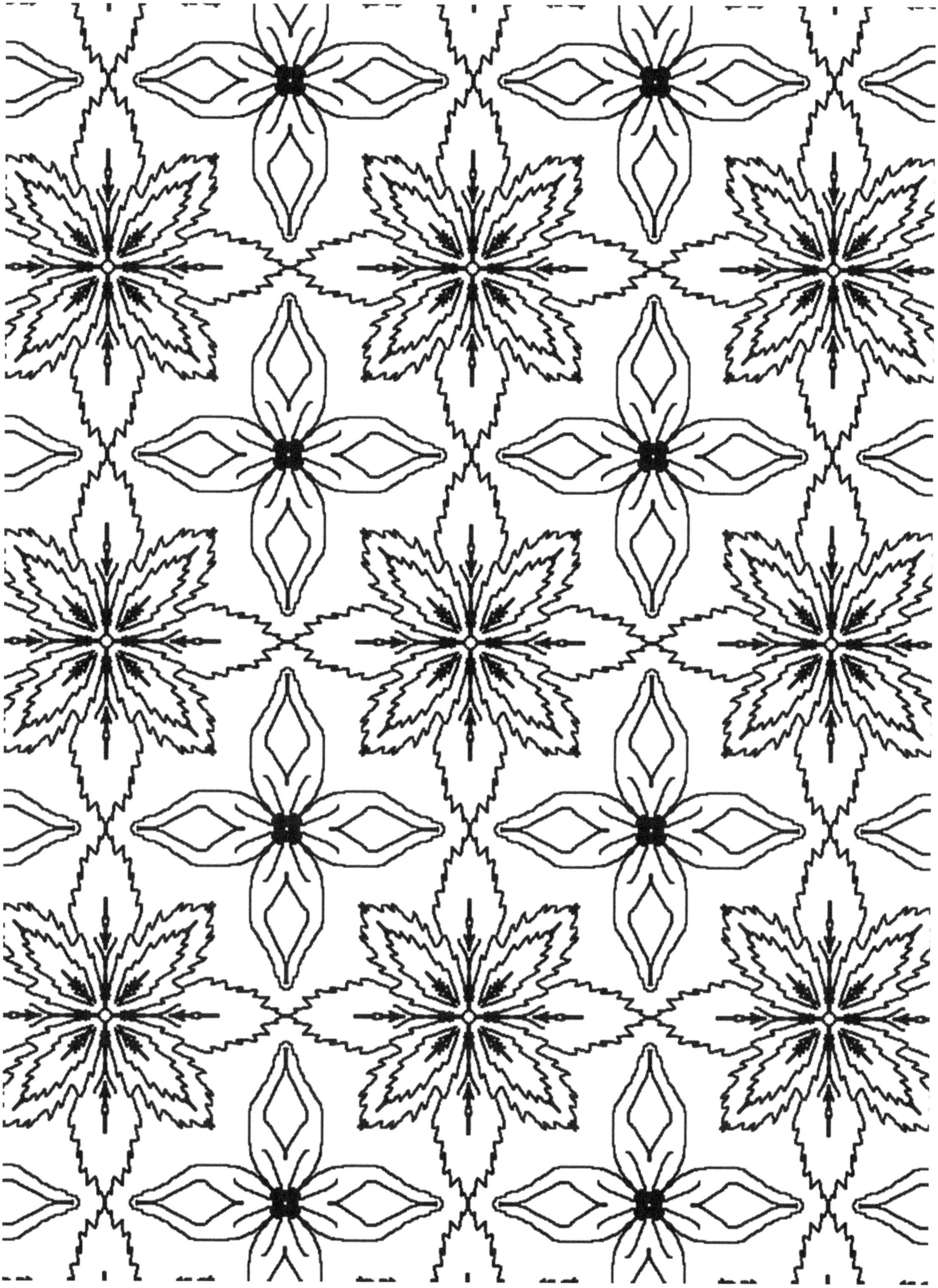

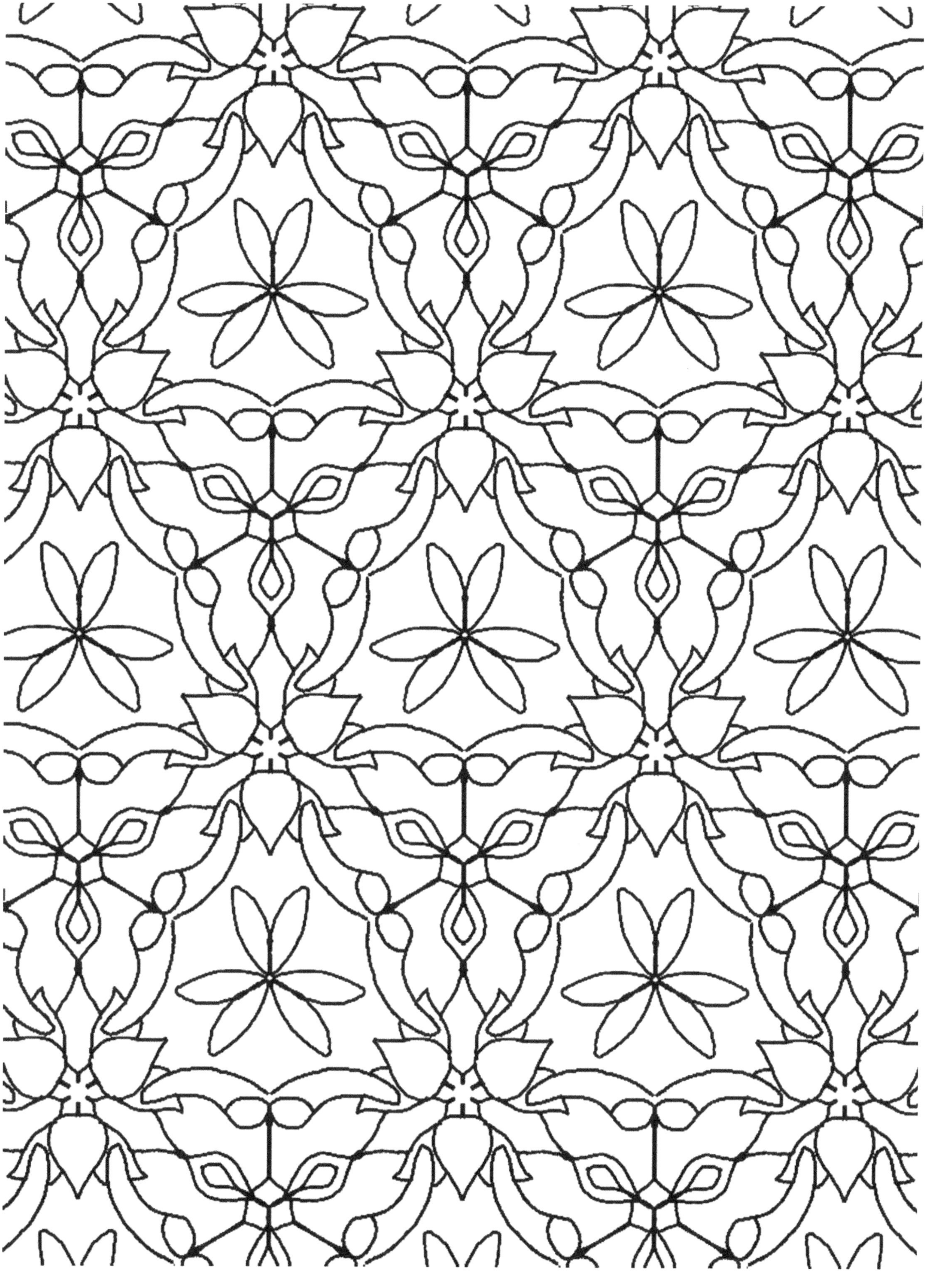

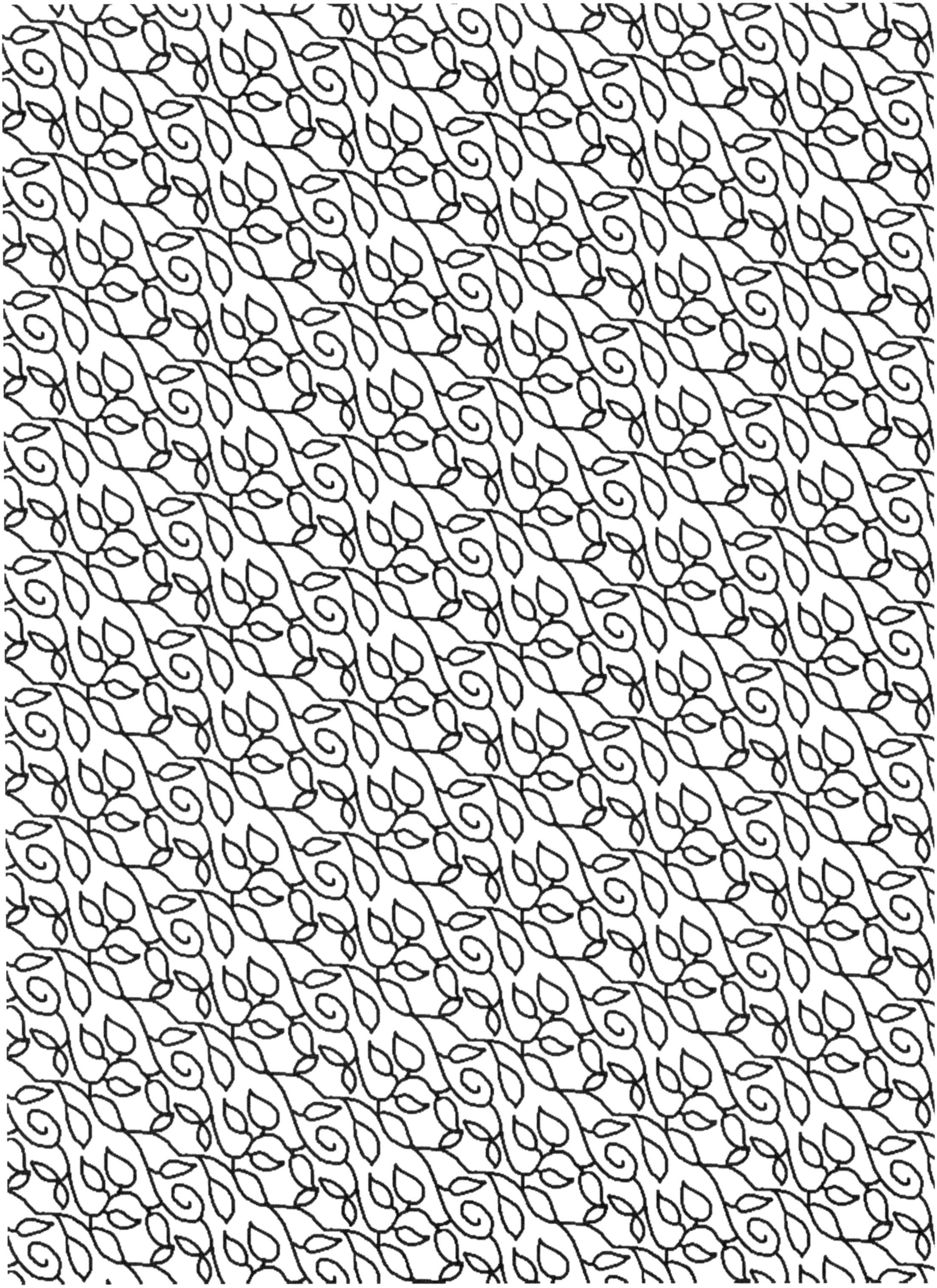

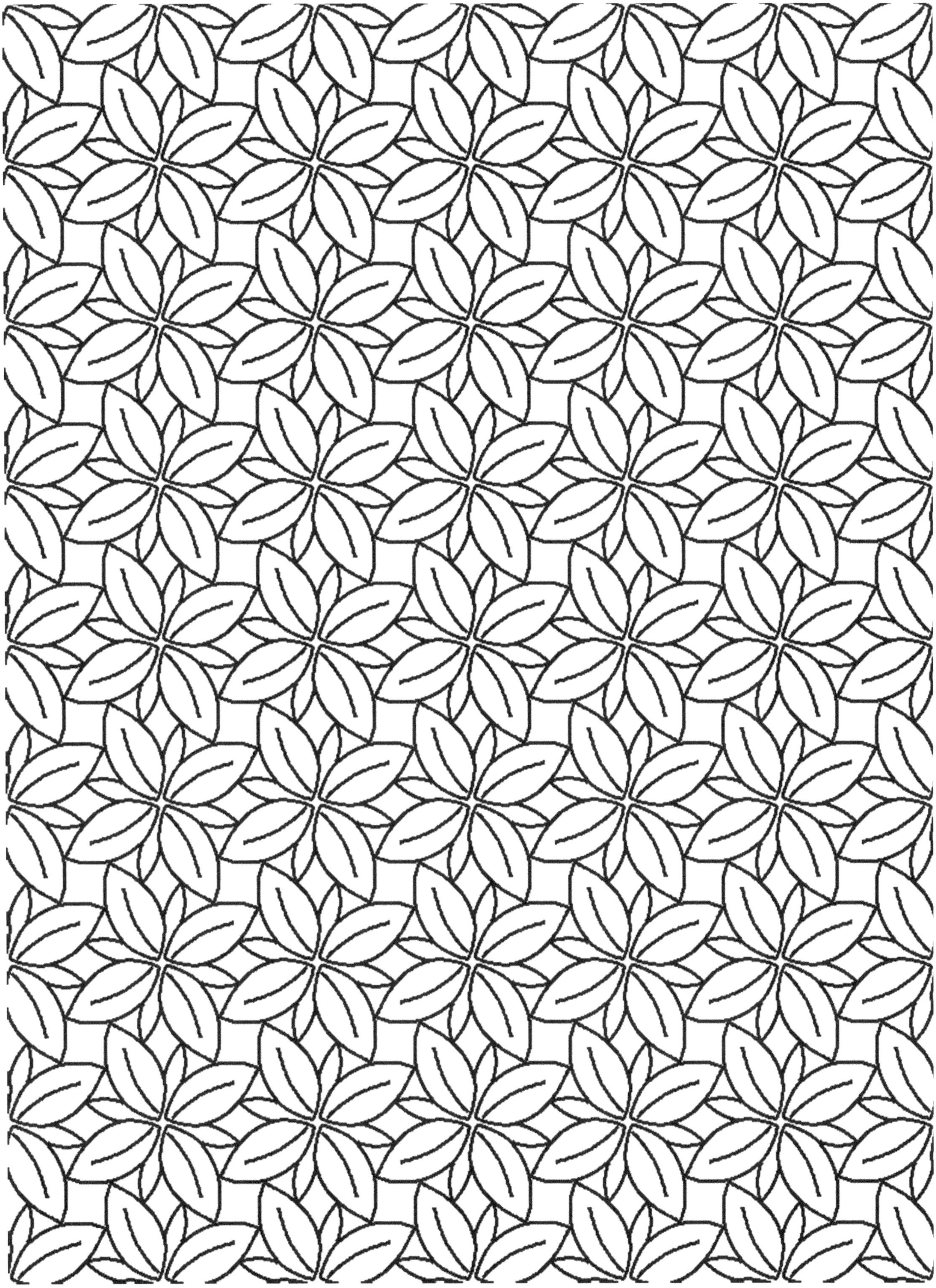

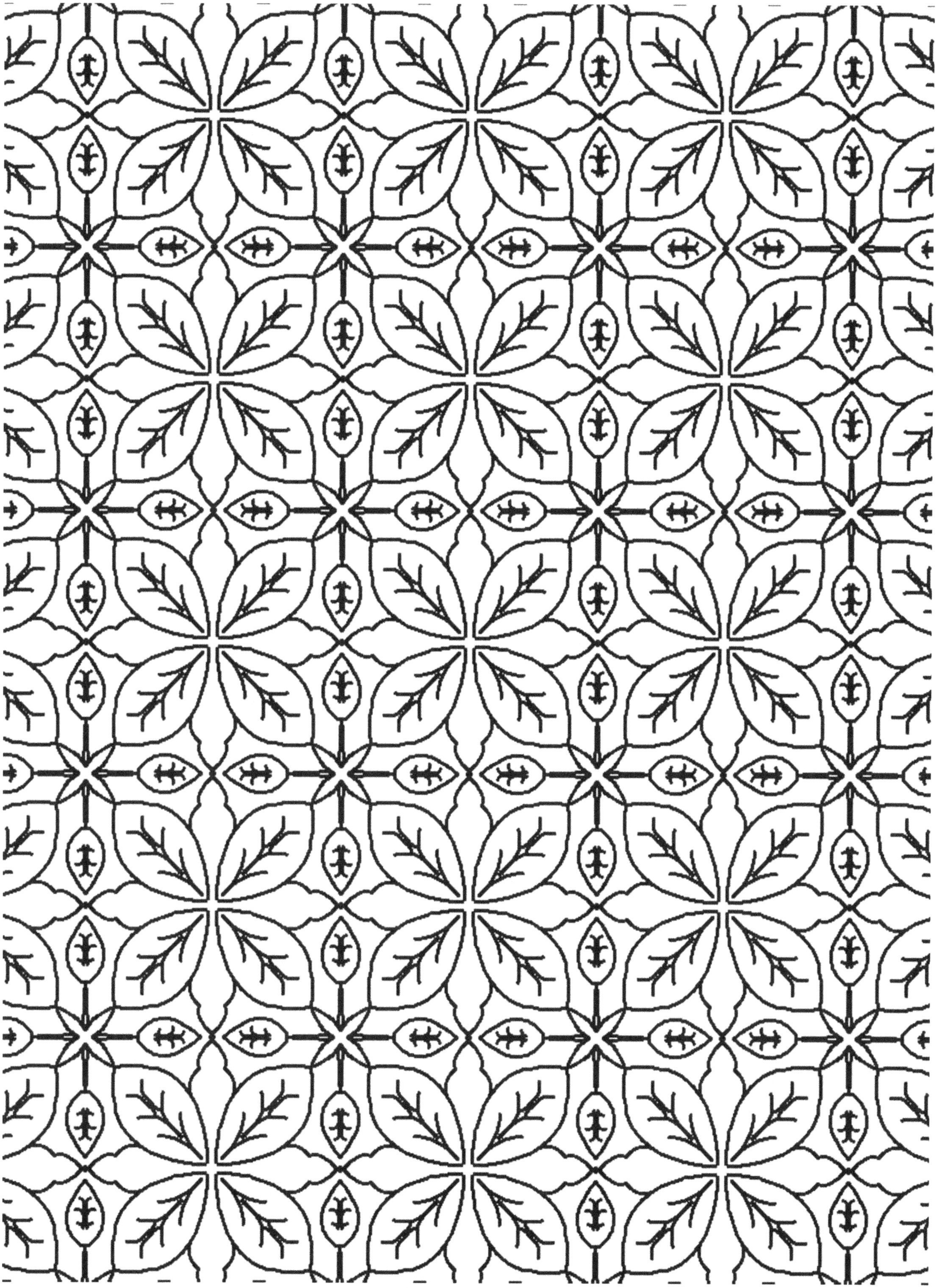

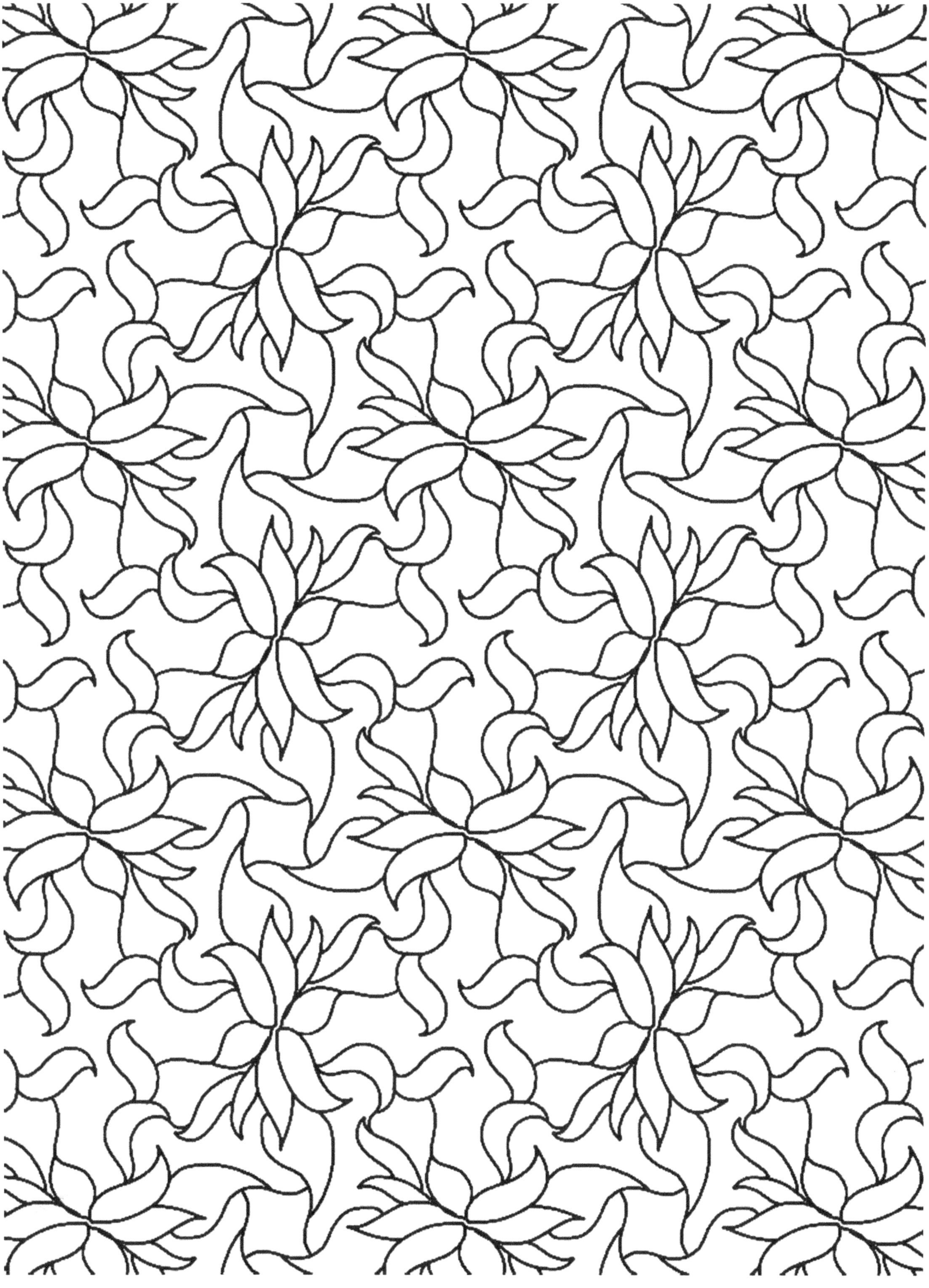

www.ingramcontent.com/pod-product-compliance
Lightning Source LLC
Chambersburg PA
CBHW081856170526
45167CB00007B/3039
* 9 7 8 1 5 4 3 0 8 9 2 4 0 *